Why Can't I Win The Lottery?....Or Something??!!

Lea Propp

ISBN: 9798328904513

PREFACE

Welcome to the adventure that is the post-COVID financial landscape, where our wallets have become as thin as a supermodel's waistline, but everything else – from bills to inflation – seems to be expanding faster than a balloon at a children's party. The pandemic has reshaped our world in countless ways, leaving many of us grappling with new financial realities and challenges. As we embark on this journey together, let's delve into the struggles, the changes, and the glimmers of hope that define our current economic climate.

Remember the good old days when "pandemic" was just a term from history books, and "lockdown" sounded like something from a prison drama? Those times feel like a distant memory. Today, we're living in the aftermath of a global event that has redefined our everyday lives and, more pointedly, our finances.

The economic impact of COVID-19 has been profound and far-reaching. For many, it meant sudden job losses, reduced hours, and the collapse of small businesses that had been nurtured for years. Governments around the world scrambled to provide support, but the reality is that financial stability for countless families was shaken to its core.

Unemployment rates spiked, savings dwindled, and for those who were lucky enough to keep their jobs, the specter of pay cuts or stalled career progress loomed large. And let's not forget the gig economy workers and freelancers, whose incomes could vanish overnight with little notice or recourse. The pandemic made one thing clear: financial security can be as fleeting as toilet paper on a supermarket shelf during a panic-buying spree.

As if shrinking wallets weren't enough, we're now facing the double whammy of rising inflation. Prices for everyday goods and services are climbing faster than the stairway to heaven, and our purchasing power is eroding at an alarming rate. Groceries, gas, rent – you name it, it's more expensive than ever.

The price hikes are everywhere, and they're relentless. It's not just that a gallon of milk or a loaf of bread costs more; it's the cumulative effect of every little increase that feels like death by a thousand cuts. It's like our money is on a diet it didn't sign up for, and we're left scrambling to adjust our budgets in ways we never imagined.

Inflation is the silent thief that sneaks into our lives, stealing our ability to save, to invest, and to feel secure about our financial future. It turns every purchase into a balancing act between necessity and luxury, often forcing tough choices on families already stretched thin. And it adds a cruel twist to the concept of cost of living, as even maintaining the same lifestyle feels increasingly out of reach.

The housing market post-COVID is a story of extremes. On one side, we have a scorching-hot seller's market where prices have skyrocketed, making homeownership a distant dream for many. Bidding wars have become the norm, and homes are selling at record speeds and prices. For those trying to buy, it feels like a rigged game where the deck is stacked against them.

On the other side, renters are facing their own set of challenges. Rental prices are climbing, and finding affordable housing is becoming akin to finding a needle in a haystack. The pandemic has exacerbated housing insecurity, pushing many into a precarious situation where the next rent payment could be the tipping point between stability and crisis.

For those who own homes, there's the unexpected boon of rising property values. But even that silver lining has a shadow – higher property taxes and the daunting task of maintaining or upgrading a home in an inflated market where even basic repairs can feel like a financial burden.

The pandemic has also shone a harsh light on the disparities in healthcare access and affordability. For many, healthcare costs have become another crushing weight on already burdened shoulders. Whether it's the high cost of health insurance, unexpected medical bills, or the ongoing expenses of managing chronic conditions, healthcare is a financial minefield that can detonate without warning.

COVID-19 itself brought a wave of medical expenses, from testing and treatments to long-term care for those dealing with lingering effects. And while vaccines have provided a path to some semblance of normalcy, the economic toll of healthcare is a persistent reminder that we're not out of the woods yet.

For families dealing with non-COVID-related health issues, the situation is equally dire. The pandemic has disrupted regular healthcare services, leading to delays in treatments and increased costs. It's a sobering reminder that our health and our financial well-being are inextricably linked, and navigating this complex landscape requires both resilience and resourcefulness.

One of the less glamorous side effects of the pandemic is the widespread disruption of global supply chains. What started as temporary shortages has morphed into a long-term crisis where "out of stock" signs are all too common, and waiting for back-ordered items has become a test of patience.

This disruption has a ripple effect on our wallets. Scarcity drives up prices, and the delays can turn everyday purchases into extravagant luxuries. Whether it's the new car that's now thousands of dollars more expensive or the household item that's been on backorder for months, the supply chain chaos adds another layer of complexity to our financial lives.

And let's not forget the impact on small businesses, which often don't have the resources to weather these supply disruptions. For many, keeping shelves stocked and customers happy has become a Herculean task, further straining finances already stretched to the breaking point.

As traditional employment took a hit, the gig economy saw an unprecedented surge. More people than ever turned to freelance work, side hustles, and gig platforms to make ends meet. This shift has brought both opportunities and challenges.

On one hand, gig work offers flexibility and the potential to supplement income quickly. It's become a lifeline for many who lost their jobs or needed to adapt to new circumstances. From driving for rideshare companies to delivering groceries, the gig economy has filled a crucial gap.

On the other hand, gig work often lacks the stability and benefits of traditional employment. There's no health insurance, no retirement plan, and no paid leave. Workers are left to navigate these uncertainties on their own, juggling multiple jobs to cobble together a livable income. The promise of flexibility comes with the reality of instability and financial precarity.

The pandemic has also accelerated the shift to remote work, transforming dining tables into desks and blurring the lines between home and office. For many, this has been a welcome change, eliminating commutes and offering more time at home. But it's also brought new financial considerations.

Working from home often means higher utility bills, more spending on home office setups, and the challenge of maintaining productivity in a space not designed for work. There's also the hidden cost of isolation and the blurring of work-life boundaries, which can take a toll on mental health and overall well-being.

For companies, the shift to remote work has sparked a re-evaluation of office space and operational costs. While some have embraced the change and reduced their physical footprint, others are grappling with the implications for company culture and employee engagement. It's a delicate balance between cost savings and maintaining a cohesive, motivated workforce.

For families with children, the pandemic has upended education and childcare arrangements, adding another layer of financial strain. Remote learning became the norm, forcing parents to juggle work, homeschooling, and childcare – often all at once. The costs of adapting to this new reality, from technology needs to tutoring, have added up quickly.

Childcare, already a significant expense for many families, became even more challenging to secure and afford. Centers closed, reopened with higher costs and limited availability, or required parents to navigate complex and often expensive backup plans. The balance between work and family life became a tightrope walk, with financial implications at every step.

The educational disruptions also highlighted the disparities in access to resources and support, particularly for lower-income families. The digital divide became more pronounced, and the costs of bridging that gap – from internet access to devices – were significant. Planning for a child's education now involves navigating a more complex and uncertain landscape.

The mental health impact of financial stress cannot be overstated. The constant worry about making ends meet, coupled with the uncertainties of the post-COVID world, has taken a toll on many. Anxiety and stress levels have soared, affecting overall well-being and productivity.

Financial difficulties often lead to a vicious cycle of stress and poor decision-making, further compounding the problem. The strain on relationships, the feeling of isolation, and the fear of an uncertain future can be overwhelming. It's a reminder that our financial health is deeply intertwined with our mental health, and addressing one requires attention to the other.

Finding ways to cope, to seek support, and to maintain a sense of humor in the face of adversity are crucial. Whether it's through community support, professional help, or simply sharing a laugh over the absurdities of our financial struggles, taking care of our mental health is a vital part of navigating these challenging times.

Despite the myriad challenges, the post-COVID financial landscape is not without its silver linings. The pandemic has prompted many of us to re-evaluate our priorities, to find new ways of living and working, and to build resilience in the face of adversity.

For some, the shift to remote work has opened up new opportunities for flexibility and work-life balance. For others, the necessity of side hustles and gig work has sparked entrepreneurial ventures and the discovery of new passions. The push towards digital transformation has expanded access to services and opportunities that were previously out of reach.

Community support and solidarity have also emerged as powerful forces. Neighbors helping neighbors, local businesses finding innovative ways to survive, and individuals stepping up to support those in need have created a sense of connection and shared purpose. It's a reminder that even in the darkest times, there's light to be found in human kindness and ingenuity.

As we look to the future, it's clear that the road to financial stability will be a complex and evolving journey. The post-COVID world presents both challenges and opportunities, and navigating it requires flexibility, creativity, and a willingness to adapt.

Building financial resilience means rethinking how we earn, save, and spend. It's about finding balance in an ever-changing landscape and making thoughtful choices that align with our goals and values. It's about leveraging new opportunities, learning from our experiences, and maintaining a sense of humor and perspective along the way.

In this book, we'll explore practical strategies, humorous insights, and real-world stories that illuminate the path forward. Whether you're grappling with shrinking wallets, rising costs, or simply trying to find joy in the journey, this guide is here to support and inspire you.

Together, we'll navigate the twists and turns of the post-COVID financial landscape, armed with knowledge, resilience, and a hearty dose of laughter. Because even when our wallets are thin, our spirits can remain rich, and our capacity for joy and connection can grow in ways we never imagined. Welcome to the journey. Let's find the silver linings, laugh at the absurdities, and build a future where we can thrive, no matter the challenges we face.

CONTENTS

ACKNOWLEDGMENTS

To all the penny pinchers, budget stretchers, and frugality aficionados out there – this one's for you!

Thank you for being the champions of thriftiness, the maestros of making-do, and the unsung heroes of financial resilience. Whether you're reusing tea bags, mastering the art of coupon clipping, or turning your spare change into a secret savings stash, you are the wizards who turn pennies into possibilities.

Your ingenuity and resourcefulness are truly inspiring. You know how to make a dollar stretch further than a yoga instructor in a contortionist competition, and you do it all with a smile (and maybe a little grumble when you see the latest prices at the gas pump). Your ability to find joy in the simple things and laugh in the face of financial adversity is nothing short of heroic.

To the masters of DIY, who can fix anything with a roll of duct tape and a can-do attitude – keep on creating! To the meal planners and bulk buyers, who turn humble ingredients into gourmet feasts – your culinary skills are legendary. And to everyone who's ever said "no" to a latte to say "yes" to their savings – you are the true MVPs of money management.

This book is a tribute to your dedication, creativity, and sense of humor. It's a celebration of finding joy in the journey, no matter how tight the budget or how daunting the challenge. Together, we navigate the ups and downs, and we do it with a wink, a nod, and a determination to make every cent count.

So here's to you, the penny pinchers of the world. May your wallets be ever light and your spirits ever lighter. Keep laughing, keep saving, and keep turning every financial challenge into a story worth telling.

With gratitude and a shared smile,

Lea Propp

WELCOME TO BROKESVILLE

Welcome to Brokesville! Population: You, Me, and every other soul who's ever looked at their bank account and wondered if it had aspirations to become a desert. Sit back, relax (though not too much, we can't afford any extra comfort), and let's embark on this delightful journey through the comical hellscape of financial struggles. Here, we'll explore the bizarre world of money – or more accurately, the lack thereof – and why, despite your fervent prayers to every conceivable deity, you're not winning the lottery anytime soon.

The Lovely Irony of Being Broke

Isn't it just grand to be broke? No, really, let's take a moment to revel in the absurdity of it all. Remember those carefree childhood days when you thought being an adult meant you could buy all the candy and toys you wanted? Surprise! Adulthood is actually a relentless game of Monopoly where the bank (which is also you) is constantly out of funds. You're not just losing; you're inventing new ways to lose. Congratulations!

You know the drill: payday arrives, and for a fleeting moment, you feel like a king or queen. But then reality checks your bank account faster than you can say "direct deposit." Bills swoop in like vultures on a carcass, and before you know it, you're left with just enough to treat yourself to a one-ply toilet paper. If you're lucky.

And then there's the endless parade of financial advice — save more, spend less, invest wisely. It's all sound logic until you realize that your biggest investment has been stockpiling instant noodles. At this point, even the thought of a financial advisor feels like a cruel joke. You'd love to save for a rainy day, but you're too busy just trying to survive the perpetual monsoon that is your life.

Let's talk about the lottery, the great American dream in the form of a tiny, scratchable rectangle. Ah, the fantasy! The thrill of imagining what you'd do with all that money. You'd quit your job, buy a mansion, travel the world, and probably hire someone to read this book to you while you bask on a private island. It's a beautiful dream. It's also about as likely as finding a unicorn in your backyard.

The cold, hard truth is, the lottery is just a tax on the mathematically challenged. Yet, every week, you find yourself standing in line at the convenience store, clutching that ticket like it's the golden key to your salvation. You know the odds are laughable, but you still think, "Hey, someone's got to win, right?" And that's how they get you — with the hope that your one-dollar investment will yield a hundred-million-dollar return. Spoiler alert: it won't.

If winning the lottery were a reasonable plan, we'd all be millionaires lounging in silk pajamas by now. But instead, here we are, marveling at how we managed to spend $200 on "essentials" at Target when we only went in for toothpaste.

Life in Brokesville is a grind. A grind that comes with a heaping side of stress and a constant sense of impending doom. You work hard, harder than you thought possible, and yet, the bills keep piling up. It's as if the universe decided to play a never-ending game of "let's see how much they can take."

Every month is a new challenge. Will you make rent? Can you afford to put gas in your car? Do you really need three meals a day? It's a juggling act, and the balls you're tossing are made of stress, anxiety, and the occasional panic attack. But hey, at least you've got a sense of humor, right? Because if you didn't laugh, you'd probably cry, and who can afford the tissues?

Financial freedom is the Holy Grail of modern life. The idea that one day, you won't have to choose between paying the electric bill and buying groceries is tantalizing. But for many of us, it feels like chasing a mirage. The closer you think you get, the farther it seems.

You've read the books, listened to the podcasts, and maybe even tried budgeting apps. But somehow, your bank balance never quite matches your aspirations. You're like Indiana Jones, if Indiana Jones was perpetually five dollars short and didn't have a whip.

But fear not! This book isn't here to lecture you on fiscal responsibility or shame you for your financial missteps. We're here to embrace the chaos and find humor in the absurdity of it all. Because if there's one thing that can get you through the endless cycle of being broke, it's laughter. And maybe, just maybe, a little bit of sarcasm.

Let's face it: life today is expensive. Everything from housing to healthcare seems to have skyrocketed in price, while wages have stayed frustratingly stagnant. The dream of owning a home feels like a cruel joke when you can barely afford rent.

And let's not even start on the cost of living in a major city. If you're lucky enough to have a job in such a place, congratulations! You've won the privilege of spending half your salary on a shoebox apartment and the other half on overpriced coffee because you need something to keep you going through the day.

Then there's the never-ending list of "essentials" that modern life demands. A smartphone? Check. Internet? Check. Streaming services because basic cable is so last century? Double check. All these add up, making you wonder if your real job is just funding your existence.

So here you are, in Brokesville, with nothing but your wit and a sense of humor to keep you afloat. It's a chaotic, unpredictable ride, but it's your ride. And as we venture through this book, we'll explore how to navigate the madness without losing your mind.

We'll laugh at the absurdity, roll our eyes at the nonsense, and find solace in knowing that you're not alone in this journey. Because at the end of the day, being broke might suck, but at least we can laugh about it together.

Welcome to Brokesville. Enjoy your stay!

1 Stretching Pennies 'Til They Scream

Welcome to Chapter 1, where we embark on the not-so-glamorous adventure of budgeting for the broke. Picture yourself as an intrepid explorer in the wild jungle of finances, armed only with your wits and a calculator. Or maybe just your wits, because who can afford a calculator? In this chapter, we'll dive into the delightful world of budgeting on a shoestring, and by "shoestring," I mean the tattered remains of one that's been repurposed for everything from tying up your pants to fixing your ancient flip-flops.

The Art of the Broke Budget

First things first, let's talk about the so-called "budget." That mythical document where income and expenses are supposed to balance out in perfect harmony. Spoiler alert: if you're here, your budget is probably more like a bad breakup – messy, painful, and full of unexpected tears. But fear not, because I'm about to share some snarky, yet surprisingly effective, tips for squeezing every last drop out of those pennies until they beg for mercy.

The Spreadsheet of Doom: Create a budget spreadsheet. No, seriously, do it. I know, it sounds about as appealing as a root canal, but trust me. Once you lay out all your expenses, you'll get to see exactly where your money is vanishing to. Plus, there's nothing quite like the joy of seeing your negative balance in 12-point Arial.

The Envelope System — Modernized: You've heard of the envelope system, right? Where you stuff cash into envelopes labeled for different expenses? Cute idea, but who uses cash anymore? Instead, set up separate bank accounts for different spending categories. One for rent, one for bills, and one for "emergency chocolate fund." And then try not to cry when the chocolate fund is empty.

The 50-30-20 Rule — Revised for the Broke: Financial gurus love the 50-30-20 rule (50% needs, 30% wants, 20% savings). But let's be real — you're not saving 20% of anything. Instead, try the 70-20-10 rule: 70% for rent and bills, 20% for food (Ramen counts as food), and 10% for everything else. Adjust as needed, because life happens and your "everything else" might just be toilet paper this month.

Subscription Audit — A Discovery in Uselessness: Go through your bank statements and cancel any subscriptions you forgot about or never use. Streaming services, magazine subscriptions, that gym membership you signed up for in a moment of delusional optimism. It's like spring cleaning for your finances, and you might find that you've been funding a small island nation's GDP with all those recurring charges.

Embrace DIY — Even When You Shouldn't: Why pay someone when you can do it yourself? Haircuts, home repairs, legal advice — what could go wrong? Sure, your bangs might end up looking like you cut them with a butter knife, and your "fixed" sink could resemble a scene from a disaster movie, but at least you're saving money. Just have a plumber and a lawyer on speed dial.

Tales of Extreme Frugality

Now that you've got a handle on the basics of budgeting (or at least you're ready to give it a shot), let's dive into the fascinating world of extreme frugality. These stories will not only entertain but might also inspire you to stretch those pennies even further. Because nothing says "I've got this" like using a tea bag more times than you can count or repurposing old socks into hand puppets for the kids' birthday party.

The Reusable Everything: Meet Jane, the queen of reusability. Jane takes frugality to new heights by reusing almost everything. Ziplock bags? Rinsed and reused. Aluminum foil? Gently wiped and reused. Christmas wrapping paper? Unwrapped with surgical precision and reused next year. Jane's house is like a museum of slightly-used objects, and she swears by her method. Who knew you could wash and reuse paper towels? Jane did.

The Grocery Store Gym: Meet Tom, a fitness enthusiast with a budget tighter than his workout pants. Instead of shelling out for a gym membership, Tom's found a unique way to stay in shape – using grocery shopping as his workout. He does lunges in the frozen food aisle, squats with bags of rice, and curls gallon jugs of milk. It's efficient, effective, and slightly terrifying for fellow shoppers.

The Zero Dollar Date Night: Sarah and Mike have mastered the art of the zero-dollar date. Forget fancy dinners and movies; these two keep their romance alive with creative, cost-free outings. From "urban foraging" for wild herbs in the park to stargazing from their apartment roof (binoculars optional), they've turned penny-pinching into an art form. Their motto? Love doesn't cost a thing – and neither does dinner if you know where to look for edible plants.

The Coupon Queen: Lily is a couponing wizard. She's that person you see at the checkout with a binder full of neatly organized coupons. Lily's turned saving money into a sport, and her pantry looks like a mini-mart stocked with items she got for next to nothing. Shampoo? Free after rebates. Pasta? Practically giving it away. She's even managed to get paid to take some items home. It's impressive, inspiring, and a little bit scary.

The Hand-Me-Down Pro: David has perfected the art of the hand-me-down. He's the youngest of four siblings and has never seen a new item of clothing in his life. But he's taken this to a whole new level. Need new furniture? David's got a cousin who's moving. Car troubles? His uncle's got an old beater he's willing to part with. David's network of family and friends is like a never-ending supply of gently-used goods. Who needs new when you can have someone else's "like new"?

Creative Money-Saving Hacks

Beyond the world of extreme frugality, there's a treasure trove of creative hacks for making your dollars stretch further than you ever thought possible. These hacks are the MacGyver solutions of the financial world – clever, unconventional, and just a bit insane. But hey, desperate times call for desperate measures, and when you're broke, every little bit helps.

The DIY Air Conditioner: Why spend hundreds on an air conditioner when you can make your own? Grab a styrofoam cooler, cut some holes in it, fill it with ice, and stick a fan on top. Voila! Instant cool air. Sure, it might look like a science experiment gone wrong, but it works – mostly. Just don't expect it to cool more than a square foot or last longer than your patience with changing the ice.

The Power of Bulk: Buying in bulk is a classic money-saving strategy, but have you ever considered buying everything in bulk? Laundry detergent, toothpaste, even toilet paper by the truckload. It might require some initial investment and a bit of storage space, but over time, you'll save a fortune. Plus, there's something oddly satisfying about knowing you have a five-year supply of Q-tips.

Turn Off the Heater, Wear a Blanket: Heating bills through the roof? Easy fix – turn off the heater and bundle up! Layering is key: sweaters, scarves, and if you're feeling really adventurous, two pairs of socks. Embrace your inner Eskimo and save big on those heating costs. Bonus points if you can knit your own blanket while wearing one.

Make Everything Last Longer: Stretched food to the limit? Try stretched toiletries. Add water to your shampoo and conditioner to make them last longer. Squeeze every last bit out of that toothpaste tube. It's like a game of "how low can you go" with your household products. Just be careful not to dilute so much that you're washing your hair with water and brushing your teeth with air.

The Plant-Based Diet: Going vegan might not just be good for your health – it can also save you money. Vegetables and grains are usually cheaper than meat and dairy. Plus, you can grow your own veggies if you've got a green thumb. Or, in my case, a brown thumb that kills everything but weeds. But hey, if you can manage it, you'll save a bundle and probably get a pat on the back from Mother Nature.

In the end, budgeting when you're broke is all about creativity, resilience, and a good sense of humor. It's about finding joy in the little victories, like making it to the end of the month with a few dollars to spare or discovering a new money-saving trick that actually works. It's about learning to live within your means, no matter how meager those means might be.

It's a tough journey, filled with challenges and frustrations, but it's also one that can teach you invaluable lessons about resourcefulness and perseverance. And if nothing else, it'll give you a treasure trove of stories to laugh about when you finally escape Brokesville. Because one day, you will. Until then, keep stretching those pennies and laughing at the absurdity of it all.

As we wrap up this chapter, remember that budgeting for the broke isn't about deprivation – it's about innovation. It's about finding new ways to thrive, even when the odds are stacked against you. So, keep those spreadsheets updated, those coupons clipped, and most importantly, keep your sense of humor intact. Because if you can laugh at your financial woes, you're already richer than you think.

2 THE MAGIC OF RAMEN

Welcome to Chapter 2, where we'll take a nostalgic trip back to your college days when Ramen noodles were your closest companion and the closest you got to gourmet was adding an egg to your instant noodles. If you've ever found yourself contemplating whether you can live off Ramen indefinitely, congratulations! You're about to become a culinary genius in the fine art of cheap eats. Grab your fork (or chopsticks if you're feeling fancy), and let's dive into the world of budget-friendly dining.

The Gourmet World of Ramen

Ah, Ramen – the quintessential symbol of frugality. It's more than just a noodle; it's a life raft in the choppy waters of financial struggle. But let's face it, eating Ramen every day can get monotonous. How do you transform this humble packet of noodles into a meal that doesn't make you question your life choices? By embracing the magic of Ramen, of course!

Ramen 101: The Basics: Let's start with the basics. You've got your brick of noodles and a packet of mystery seasoning. Perfect. Boil some water, toss in the noodles, add the seasoning, and you've got dinner. But that's just the beginning. Think of Ramen as a blank canvas, waiting for your culinary artistry to transform it.

Upgrade with Add-Ins: The secret to making Ramen more bearable (and dare I say, delicious?) lies in the add-ins. Scour your fridge and pantry for anything that might give your noodles a boost. Leftover veggies? Toss them in. An egg? Crack it open and let it poach in the broth. Have a packet of soy sauce or some sriracha? Add them for an extra kick. Suddenly, your bowl of

11

Ramen is looking more like a meal and less like a last resort.

Ramen Stir-Fry: If you're feeling adventurous, try turning your Ramen into a stir-fry. Cook the noodles as usual, then drain them and toss them in a hot pan with a splash of oil. Add whatever veggies or proteins you have on hand – think frozen peas, shredded carrots, or leftover chicken. Stir-fry everything together with a dash of soy sauce, and voila! You've just leveled up your Ramen game.

Ramen Souped Up: For a heartier meal, transform your Ramen into a soup. Use broth instead of water, and add in some canned beans, frozen corn, and a handful of spinach. This isn't just Ramen; it's a hearty, satisfying bowl of soup that's cheap and cheerful. You might even convince yourself you're dining in a trendy noodle bar. Almost.

Ramen Salad: When you're tired of hot noodles, consider a cold Ramen salad. Cook and cool the noodles, then mix them with a tangy dressing and whatever fresh veggies you have. Cabbage, carrots, and cucumbers work great. Top with some peanuts or sesame seeds for crunch. It's like a picnic in a bowl, minus the ants and the sunshine.

Surviving on a Tight Food Budget

Living on a tight food budget doesn't mean you have to eat like a caveman (unless you're into that sort of thing). With a little creativity and planning, you can stretch your dollars further than you ever thought possible. Here are some comical yet practical tips to help you navigate the world of budget-friendly eating.

The $20 Challenge: Set yourself a challenge to spend no more than $20 a week on groceries. It's like a game show, except the prize is the ability to eat without crying. Focus on buying staple items that can be used in multiple meals – rice, beans, pasta, and of course, Ramen. Bonus points if you can throw in a fresh vegetable or two without going over budget.

Bulk Up Your Meals: Learn the art of bulking up your meals. Add rice or pasta to your soups to make them more filling. Mix beans or lentils into your casseroles. These cheap, filling additions will help you stretch your meals further and keep you fuller longer. Plus, they add a bit of variety to your otherwise monotonous diet.

Embrace the Power of Potatoes: Potatoes are your best friend. They're cheap, versatile, and filling. Bake them, mash them, roast them, or turn them into fries. You can even make a giant batch of potato soup and live off it for days. And if you get really desperate, you can always use them to power a small lightbulb. But let's hope it doesn't come to that.

Freezer Frenzy: Your freezer is a treasure trove of possibilities. Freeze leftovers for quick meals later on. Stock up on frozen veggies when they're on sale. You can even freeze bread to prevent it from going moldy before you finish it. Think of your freezer as a time capsule of food, saving you from future hunger pangs.

Grocery Store Games: Turn your grocery shopping into a game. See how many discount items you can find. Challenge yourself to make a meal out of whatever's on sale. Or play "Guess the Total" at the checkout – closest to the actual total without going over wins. The prize? The satisfaction of not having to put anything back. It's fun and frugal!

Cheap Eats: Recipes to Save Your Sanity

Now that you've got the basics down, it's time to put them into action. Here are some entertaining recipes and tips to make your cheap meals not just bearable, but genuinely enjoyable. These aren't just meals; they're culinary adventures on a shoestring budget.

The Ultimate Ramen Omelette:

1. **Ingredients**: 1 pack of Ramen, 2 eggs, any veggies or meat you have.
2. **Instructions**: Cook the Ramen and drain it. Beat the eggs and mix in the Ramen, veggies, and meat. Pour the mixture into a hot, greased pan and cook until the eggs are set. Fold in half and serve. Congratulations, you've just made an omelette that's part noodle, part egg, and all delicious.

Beans & Rice — But Make It Fun:

1. **Ingredients**: 1 can of beans, 1 cup of rice, 1 onion, spices.
2. **Instructions**: Cook the rice according to the package. Sauté the onion until it's golden. Add the beans (drained and rinsed) and spices to the pan. Mix with the rice and cook until everything is warm. This classic combo is a staple for a reason — it's cheap, filling, and surprisingly tasty. For extra flair, add a dollop of salsa or a sprinkle of cheese (if you're feeling fancy).

Pasta Primavera – The Budget Version:

1. **Ingredients**: 1 box of pasta, 1 bag of frozen mixed vegetables, 1 jar of cheap pasta sauce.
2. **Instructions**: Cook the pasta and drain. Microwave or boil the veggies. Mix everything together with the pasta sauce. It's like dining at a fancy Italian restaurant, if that restaurant had a strict $5 budget and a penchant for frozen produce.

Peanut Butter Banana Toast:

1. **Ingredients**: Bread, peanut butter, 1 banana.
2. **Instructions**: Toast the bread. Spread with peanut butter. Slice the banana and arrange it artfully on top. It's a breakfast fit for a king – or at least, a very frugal monarch. For an extra touch of elegance, drizzle with a bit of honey or sprinkle with cinnamon.

The Not-So-Sad Salad:

1. **Ingredients**: Whatever fresh or leftover veggies you have, a can of beans, a basic dressing (oil, vinegar, salt, and pepper).
2. **Instructions**: Chop the veggies and toss them in a bowl. Drain and rinse the beans, and add them to the mix. Dress with the oil and vinegar. This is a salad that's anything but sad. It's colorful, crunchy, and a great way to use up those odds and ends in your fridge.

The Art of Making Cheap Meals Bearable

Eating on a tight budget doesn't have to be a miserable experience. With a bit of creativity and a sense of humor, you can make even the cheapest meals something to look forward to. Here are some tips to keep your meals enjoyable, no matter how limited your budget.

Presentation is Key: Even the simplest meal can feel special if you present it well. Use your fanciest (or only) plate. Arrange your food neatly. Light a candle if you have one. It's all about tricking your brain into thinking you're dining in style, even if you're just eating beans and rice for the third time this week.

Spice It Up: Spices are the easiest way to add flavor to any meal. Stock up on basics like salt, pepper, garlic powder, and chili flakes. They're cheap and can transform bland food into something exciting. Experiment with different combinations until you find your favorite. Who knew that a sprinkle of paprika could make your scrambled eggs taste gourmet?

Batch Cooking: Save time and money by cooking in batches. Make a big pot of soup, chili, or stew and portion it out for the week. Not only does this save you from cooking every day, but it also gives you a ready-to-go meal when you're too tired to even think about cooking. And let's be honest, that's most days.

Embrace the Leftovers: Don't let anything go to waste. Get creative with your leftovers. Turn yesterday's roast chicken into today's chicken salad. Transform that extra pasta into a frittata. With a bit of imagination, leftovers can become a whole new meal. It's like recycling, but tastier.

Cook with Friends: If you can, try cooking with friends. Pool your resources and cook a big meal together. Not only does this make the food go further, but it also makes the process more enjoyable. Plus, you get to sample dishes you might not have thought to make yourself. And if all else fails, there's always the possibility of someone else's cooking mishap making yours look like a Michelin-starred creation.

Finding Joy in the Small Things

At the end of the day, surviving on a tight food budget is about finding joy in the small things. It's about appreciating the creativity that comes with making something out of nothing. It's about laughing at the absurdity of it all and knowing that even in the toughest times, you can still find moments of delight.

So, embrace the magic of Ramen, the power of potatoes, and the endless possibilities of beans and rice. Celebrate the small victories, like discovering a new favorite recipe or mastering the art of cooking with what you have. And most importantly, keep your sense of humor. Because in the world of budget-friendly dining, laughter is the best seasoning.

3 DIY DELIGHTS

Welcome to Chapter 3, where we delve into the wonderful, chaotic, and occasionally disastrous world of DIY. In a perfect world, we'd all be able to hire professionals for everything from home repairs to haircuts. But in Brokesville, the perfect world is just a fairy tale, and we're left to fend for ourselves with duct tape, YouTube tutorials, and a can-do attitude. So, grab your toolkit (or whatever passes for one), and let's embark on this hilarious journey of doing everything yourself.

> *Disclaimer: While our DIY suggestions are meant to inspire and entertain, they come with a friendly warning. Always do your research before starting any project. Check out YouTube tutorials, Pinterest boards, and reputable DIY blogs for detailed instructions and safety tips. We don't want you wasting money or, heaven forbid, putting yourself in harm's way. Think of this chapter as a humorous guide to the potential wonders (and pitfalls) of DIY, not as a professional manual.*

The Joy of Doing It Yourself (Sort Of)

The essence of DIY is not just about saving money – it's about the thrill of taking on tasks you have no business attempting and emerging (hopefully) unscathed. Whether you're fixing a leaky faucet or cutting your own hair, DIY is a blend of bravery, stubbornness, and a touch of insanity. Let's explore some sarcastic suggestions for becoming your own jack-of-all-trades, whether you want to or not.

Haircuts at Home – Scissors Optional:

Why spend money at a salon when you can snip away at your own locks in the comfort of your bathroom? Sure, professional haircuts might leave you looking like a movie star, but DIY haircuts will leave you with a unique style that says, "I did this myself, and it shows." Armed with a pair of kitchen scissors and a YouTube video titled "Easy DIY Haircuts," you're ready to transform your look. Just remember, hair grows back. Eventually.

Plumbing Problems? No Problem!:

A clogged sink or a running toilet is no match for the fearless DIYer. Why call a plumber when you can tackle the problem with a plunger, a wrench, and sheer determination? After all, how hard can it be? A few twists here, a little bit of elbow grease there, and you'll have water spraying everywhere in no time. The key is to act like you know what you're doing and hope for the best. And maybe keep a mop handy.

The Art of Self-Taught Home Repairs:

Your home is a canvas, and every repair is a brushstroke. Whether it's fixing a hole in the drywall or rewiring a light switch, you've got this. Just remember, all you need is some spackle, a screwdriver, and a lot of optimism. And when in doubt, just cover it with a strategically placed picture or piece of furniture. It's like hiding your problems in plain sight.

Gardening: Growing Your Own Food (Or Not):

Who needs a green thumb when you've got the internet? Transform your backyard (or windowsill) into a bountiful garden that provides endless produce – or at least a few scraggly herbs. Grab some seeds, throw them in some dirt, and water occasionally. Voila! Instant gardener. And if things don't grow, just tell people you're cultivating a wild, natural aesthetic.

Clothing Alterations: Sewing for the Brave:

Hemming your own pants or sewing on a button can save you a fortune on tailor fees. Dust off that old sewing kit and give it a go. If you can manage to thread the needle without losing your sanity, you're halfway there. And if your stitches aren't quite straight or your alterations go awry, just call it "customized fashion." After all, it's the imperfections that make it unique.

DIY Triumphs: Victories Against All Odds

Despite the challenges, there's a certain joy in the triumphs of DIY. Every successful project is a testament to your ingenuity and perseverance. Let's celebrate some stories of DIY victories that prove anything is possible with a little creativity and a lot of grit.

The Makeshift Patio Furniture:

Meet Alex, who decided that buying new patio furniture was an unnecessary expense. Instead, he collected old pallets from the local hardware store and, with a bit of sanding and some leftover paint, transformed them into a charming outdoor seating area. It might not be quite as comfortable as store-bought furniture, but it's sturdy, functional, and has that rustic charm that says, "I did this myself, and I didn't spend a dime."

The DIY Home Gym:

Gym memberships can be pricey, so Maria decided to create her own workout space at home. Armed with some resistance bands, a yoga mat, and a set of mismatched dumbbells she found at a garage sale, she set up a mini-gym in her garage. She even made her own weights using sand-filled milk jugs. Now, she's in the best shape of her life and didn't have to spend a fortune on fancy equipment.

The Backyard Chicken Coop:

Inspired by the farm-to-table movement, Tom built a chicken coop in his backyard. Using recycled materials and a basic blueprint from the internet, he constructed a cozy home for a few hens. Not only does he get fresh eggs every morning, but he's also become the go-to guy in his neighborhood for chicken advice. It's a win-win, except for the part where the chickens occasionally escape and wreak havoc on his garden.

The Homemade Beauty Salon:

Tired of spending money on beauty treatments, Jane took matters into her own hands. She started making her own face masks, hair treatments, and even nail polish. Using ingredients like honey, coconut oil, and baking soda, she's created a whole line of DIY beauty products. Her friends now come to her for beauty tips and treatments, and she hasn't stepped foot in a salon in years.

The Recycled Home Decor:

Lisa has a knack for turning trash into treasure. She's made picture frames from old window panes, turned wine bottles into vases, and even created a chandelier from recycled spoons. Her home is a testament to her creativity and resourcefulness, filled with unique pieces that are both stylish and eco-friendly. Plus, she's saved a fortune on home decor.

DIY Disasters: Laughing Through the Chaos

For every DIY triumph, there's a disaster waiting in the wings. These stories remind us that not every project goes according to plan, and sometimes, things go hilariously wrong. But even in failure, there's something to be learned – or at least a good story to tell.

The Haircut from Hell:

Ben decided to save money by cutting his own hair. Armed with a pair of scissors and some misplaced confidence, he started snipping away. Halfway through, he realized he had no idea what he was doing. The result was a lopsided mess that looked like it had been attacked by a weed whacker. He ended up shaving his head and wearing a hat for weeks. The moral? Some things are better left to the professionals.

The Plumbing Fiasco:

Sara thought fixing a leaky faucet would be a breeze. After watching a few DIY videos, she felt ready to tackle the job. But as soon as she started, water began spraying everywhere. She tried tightening this and loosening that, but nothing worked. By the end of the day, her kitchen was flooded, and she had to call in a professional. The repair cost twice as much as it would have if she'd called the plumber in the first place. Lesson learned: sometimes, it's okay to admit defeat.

The Home Improvement Horror:

Jack wanted to replace a broken tile in his bathroom. How hard could it be? He pried up the old tile, but in the process, managed to crack several surrounding tiles. Undeterred, he decided to replace them all. Hours of frustration later, he was surrounded by a pile of broken tiles, dried cement on his hands, and a bathroom floor that looked worse than when he started. In the end, he gave up and hired a handyman to fix his mess.

The Garden That Never Grew:

Emily dreamed of a lush vegetable garden that would supply her with fresh produce all summer. She planted seeds with high hopes, but despite her best efforts, nothing grew. Weeks passed, and her garden remained a barren patch of dirt. Turns out, she had planted in the wrong season, and the soil was too poor for anything to thrive. She eventually gave up and settled for a few potted herbs on her windowsill. Gardening, it seems, is harder than it looks.

The Clothing Catastrophe:

Chris tried his hand at sewing his own clothes. His first project was a simple pair of shorts. How hard could it be? He measured, cut, and sewed with enthusiasm. But when he tried them on, he realized he'd sewn the legs together wrong. Instead of shorts, he had a confusing, unwearable garment that defied explanation. He learned that tailoring is an art, one that he was not destined to master.

Embracing the DIY Spirit

Despite the challenges and occasional disasters, there's something empowering about the DIY approach. It's about taking control, learning new skills, and finding creative solutions to problems. It's about turning "I can't afford to pay for that" into "I can do that myself." And even when things go wrong, there's a certain satisfaction in knowing you gave it your best shot.

Start Small: If you're new to DIY, start with small projects. Try simple tasks like hanging a picture frame or assembling a piece of flat-pack furniture. These little victories will build your confidence and skills for tackling bigger projects.

Learn from Mistakes: Every disaster is a learning opportunity. Don't be discouraged by failure. Instead, take it as a chance to improve and do better next time. Remember, even the most skilled DIYers had to start somewhere, and mistakes are part of the journey.

Use the Right Tools: Having the right tools makes a world of difference. Invest in some basic equipment, like a good screwdriver set, a hammer, and a pair of pliers. These will serve you well in a variety of projects and save you from unnecessary frustration.

Know Your Limits: While the DIY spirit is about pushing boundaries, it's also important to know when to call in a professional. Some tasks, like electrical work or major plumbing repairs, are best left to those with the proper training. There's no shame in admitting when you're out of your depth.

Celebrate Your Successes: Every completed project, no matter how small, is a victory. Take pride in your accomplishments, and use them as motivation to keep going. Whether it's fixing a leaky faucet or building a piece of furniture, you've achieved something worth celebrating.

__You will find more ideas at the end of this book__

Finding Humor in the Chaos

The world of DIY is filled with ups and downs, triumphs and disasters. It's a rollercoaster ride of creativity, frustration, and occasional hilarity. Through it all, the most important thing is to keep your sense of humor. Laugh at your mistakes, enjoy your successes, and remember that even the worst DIY disaster is a story worth telling.

So, embrace the chaos. Grab your tools, roll up your sleeves, and dive into your next project with enthusiasm and a healthy dose of sarcasm. Because in the end, the journey is just as important as the destination, and sometimes, the mess you make along the way is half the fun.

4 SIDE HUSTLES AND GIGGLES

Welcome to, where we dive into the world of side hustles and gig economy jobs, all designed to put a little extra cash in your pocket without losing your sanity (or your sense of humor). Whether you're looking to supplement your income or just want a reason to get out of the house and interact with humans, this chapter is your guide to the wacky and wonderful world of side gigs. So, let's explore some funny, quirky, and downright bizarre ways to make money on the side.

Funny Ideas for Side Jobs and Gigs

Side hustles are like the Swiss Army knives of employment – versatile, handy, and sometimes a bit ridiculous. Here are some humorous ideas for side jobs that might just be the perfect fit for your unique skills and interests.

Dog Walking: Your Daily Dose of Exercise (and Poop Scooping):

If you love dogs and don't mind a little (okay, a lot of) poop, dog walking is a great way to earn some extra cash. Imagine getting paid to stroll through the neighborhood, enjoying the fresh air and furry companionship. Just be prepared for the occasional tug-of-war with a particularly enthusiastic pup or the mortifying moment when you realize you've been trailing a poop bag for blocks.

Mystery Shopping: The Job Where Paranoia Pays Off:

Ever wanted to get paid for shopping? Mystery shopping is your chance to play detective in your local stores. You'll be tasked with evaluating customer service, product displays, and cleanliness, all while trying to look inconspicuous. It's like being James Bond, but with less espionage and more note-taking. Just try not to blow your cover by whispering, "The eagle has landed," to yourself in the cereal aisle.

Pet Sitting: Your Ticket to a Furry Staycation:

Pet sitting combines the joy of caring for animals with the comfort of being in someone else's home. It's like a mini-vacation with a furry twist. You get to cuddle with cats, play with dogs, and maybe even try your hand at feeding exotic fish or birds. The catch? You have to remember which food goes in which bowl and which door leads to the litter box.

Freelance Writing: Crafting Words for Dollars:

If you've got a knack for words and a strong internet connection, freelance writing might be your golden ticket. You can write articles, blog posts, or even product descriptions, all from the comfort of your own home. The upside? You get to work in your pajamas. The downside? You might find yourself writing a 1,000-word piece on the virtues of biodegradable toilet paper at 3 AM.

Driving for Rideshare: The Road to Extra Cash:

Driving for a rideshare service like Uber or Lyft can be a fun way to make money if you enjoy chatting with strangers and navigating city traffic. You'll meet a variety of passengers, from the overly chatty to the ones who treat your car like a confessional. Just remember to stock up on gum and water, and prepare for the occasional late-night request to the Taco Bell drive-thru.

Tutoring: Sharing Your Wisdom (or Faking It):

If you're knowledgeable in a particular subject, tutoring can be a lucrative side hustle. Help students with math, science, or even foreign languages. The best part? You get to feel like a genius for an hour. The challenge? Explaining algebra to a teenager who'd rather be anywhere else. Bonus points if you can keep a straight face while using real-world examples like calculating the probability of winning the lottery (hint: it's low).

House Sitting: Living the Life of Luxury (Sort Of):

House sitting is like playing house in someone else's mansion. You get to water plants, check the mail, and bask in the glory of a well-stocked fridge. It's the perfect gig if you enjoy peace and quiet and pretending you're living in a different tax bracket. Just don't get too comfortable – you still have to clean up before the homeowners return.

Voiceover Work: Becoming the Next Morgan Freeman:

Have a smooth, mellifluous voice? Voiceover work could be your calling. Lend your voice to commercials, audiobooks, or even video games. It's an ideal job for those who love talking and want to get paid for it. The downside? You might spend hours perfecting the pronunciation of "gluten-free, organic quinoa" for a 30-second ad.

Handyman (or Handywoman) Services: Fixing What Others Can't:

If you're good with tools and love solving problems, offering handyman services can be a rewarding side gig. Fix leaky faucets, assemble furniture, or patch up drywall. The thrill of the job? Seeing the relief on people's faces when you fix something they thought was beyond repair. The downside? The occasional encounter with a spider the size of a small dog hiding behind a leaky pipe.

Online Marketplaces: Selling Your (Unwanted) Treasures:

Turn your clutter into cash by selling items on online marketplaces like eBay or Facebook Marketplace. Whether it's old clothes, electronics, or that weird lamp your aunt gave you, there's a buyer out there somewhere. The best part? You get to practice your sales pitch and negotiation skills. The worst part? Realizing you sold your vintage vinyl collection for less than the cost of a latte.

The Pros and Cons of Various Side Hustles

Every side hustle comes with its own set of perks and pitfalls. Let's take a humorous look at the pros and cons of some popular side gigs, so you can decide which one (or ones) are worth your time and effort.

Dog Walking:

1. **Pros**: Fresh air, exercise, and canine cuddles. You get to be a dog's best friend and get paid for it. Plus, dogs never complain about your choice of music.
2. **Cons**: Picking up poop, rain or shine. And the occasional runaway dog that decides to chase a squirrel across a busy street. Also, trying to convince a 100-pound Great Dane that, no, it really doesn't need to drag you through the mud.

Mystery Shopping:

1. **Pros**: Getting paid to shop and evaluate services. You get to feel like a secret agent on a mission. Plus, you might score some free samples or discounts.
2. **Cons**: Trying to act natural while taking mental notes on the cleanliness of the restroom. Also, the crushing realization that even when you're being paid to shop, you still can't afford to buy anything.

Pet Sitting:

1. **Pros**: The joy of spending time with animals and staying in a different environment. It's like a mini-vacation with furry friends.
2. **Cons**: Remembering feeding schedules, cleaning litter boxes, and dealing with pets that have separation anxiety. And let's not forget the joy of removing hairballs from your shoes.

Freelance Writing:

1. **Pros**: Flexibility to work from anywhere and the satisfaction of seeing your name in print. You get to explore different topics and sharpen your writing skills.
2. **Cons**: Dealing with writer's block, demanding clients, and the constant battle to get paid on time. Also, the occasional existential crisis at 2 AM about why you're writing a blog post about "10 Ways to Organize Your Sock Drawer."

Rideshare Driving:

1. **Pros**: Meeting new people, flexible hours, and getting paid to drive around town. You can even listen to your favorite podcasts while working.
2. **Cons**: Navigating traffic, dealing with rude passengers, and cleaning up after someone's late-night party in your backseat. And don't forget the joy of explaining why you can't take them to their "secret" club that's totally not on the map.

Tutoring:

1. **Pros**: Helping others learn and the satisfaction of seeing a student's "aha" moment. You get to reinforce your own knowledge and maybe even learn something new.
2. **Cons**: Explaining the same concept multiple times in different ways and dealing with distracted or disinterested students. And the delightful experience of trying to convince a teenager that math is, indeed, useful in real life.

House Sitting:

1. **Pros**: Enjoying someone else's home and amenities without the responsibility. You get to play house in a new environment and maybe even use a pool.
2. **Cons**: Keeping everything in order, dealing with unexpected home issues, and the occasional panic attack when you think you left the front door unlocked. Plus, trying to figure out how to work their complicated coffee maker without calling tech support.

Voiceover Work:

1. **Pros**: Using your voice to bring scripts to life and working from home. You get to be the voice behind commercials, audiobooks, and more.
2. **Cons**: Long hours in a recording booth, editing your own audio, and the joy of repeating the same line 50 times to get it just right. And realizing you now hate the sound of your own voice.

Handyman Services:

1. **Pros**: Fixing things and helping people solve problems. You get to use your hands, learn new skills, and see the tangible results of your work.
2. **Cons**: Dealing with unexpected challenges, such as discovering a nest of spiders in a wall or a pipe that won't stop leaking. And the occasional moment of sheer panic when you realize you've just made the problem worse.

Online Marketplaces:

1. **Pros**: Turning unwanted items into cash and decluttering your home. You get to set your own prices and negotiate with buyers.
2. **Cons**: Dealing with lowball offers, no-show buyers, and the hassle of packing and shipping items. Plus, the crushing disappointment when you realize your treasured Beanie Baby collection is worth less than a cup of coffee.

The Fun and Challenges of Side Hustles

Side hustles can be a great way to earn extra money, learn new skills, and meet interesting people. They can also be a source of stress, frustration, and hilarious stories. Here's a look at the lighter side of juggling multiple gigs and the challenges that come with them.

The Balancing Act:

Managing a side hustle alongside your main job can feel like juggling flaming torches while riding a unicycle. You have to keep everything in balance without dropping the ball (or setting your hair on fire). But with a bit of practice and a lot of caffeine, you can find a rhythm that works for you.

The Unexpected Perks:

Every side hustle comes with its own unexpected perks. Whether it's the joy of a dog's wagging tail, the satisfaction of a well-written article, or the thrill of a successful sale, these little moments make all the effort worthwhile. Plus, you get some great stories to share at parties.

The Importance of Boundaries:

When you're working multiple gigs, setting boundaries is crucial. It's easy to let your side hustle take over your life, but it's important to make time for yourself and your loved ones. After all, you're hustling to improve your life, not to burn out. And remember, it's okay to say no sometimes.

The Community of Hustlers:

One of the best parts of the side hustle world is the community of fellow hustlers. Whether you're sharing tips with other dog walkers, commiserating with freelance writers, or swapping stories with rideshare drivers, there's a sense of camaraderie that makes the journey a bit easier and a lot more fun.

The Lessons Learned:

Every side hustle teaches you something new. You'll learn how to manage your time, deal with different types of people, and handle unexpected challenges. These skills aren't just valuable for your side gigs – they'll also benefit you in your main job and your personal life. Plus, you'll gain a newfound appreciation for anyone who does these jobs full-time.

Making the Most of Your Side Hustle

To get the most out of your side hustle, it's important to approach it with the right mindset. Here are some tips to help you thrive in the gig economy and turn your side job into a source of joy, not just income.

Choose Something You Enjoy:

If you're going to spend your free time working, make sure it's something you enjoy. Whether it's walking dogs, writing, or tinkering with gadgets, find a side hustle that aligns with your interests and passions. This way, it won't feel like work – it'll feel like a hobby that happens to pay you.

Set Realistic Goals:

Be clear about why you're doing a side hustle and what you hope to achieve. Whether it's saving for a vacation, paying off debt, or just having extra spending money, set realistic goals that keep you motivated. And don't be afraid to adjust them as needed – flexibility is key.

Stay Organized:

Juggling multiple gigs requires good organization. Keep track of your schedules, finances, and deadlines to avoid burnout and confusion. Use tools like calendars, spreadsheets, and apps to stay on top of everything. And remember, it's okay to take a break when you need it.

Network and Learn:

Connect with others in your side hustle community. Share tips, ask for advice, and learn from their experiences. The gig economy is full of people who are happy to help and support each other. Plus, networking can lead to new opportunities and collaborations.

Have Fun and Enjoy the Ride:

Most importantly, have fun! Side hustles are a great way to explore new interests, meet new people, and challenge yourself. Embrace the ups and downs, laugh at the absurdities, and enjoy the journey. After all, life is too short to take too seriously – especially when you're hustling on the side.

5 SURVIVING FINANCIAL FAILS

Welcome to, where we embrace the chaos of financial fails with a hearty laugh and a knowing nod. We've all been there – that sinking feeling when you realize you've made a financial blunder of epic proportions. Whether it's blowing your budget on impulse buys or investing in a "sure thing" that turned out to be anything but, financial missteps are part of the journey. The key is to find humor in the mess and learn from the experience. So, let's dive into some hilarious accounts of financial fails and uncover tips for laughing through the struggles.

Hilarious Accounts of Financial Missteps

We all have our stories of financial disasters – those moments when our wallets screamed in agony, and our bank accounts wept. Here are some rib-tickling tales of financial missteps that remind us we're not alone in our money mishaps.

The Infamous Latte Budget Blunder:

Meet Emma, who decided to get serious about her finances. She meticulously planned her budget, accounting for every dollar. Her Achilles' heel? Her love for gourmet lattes. She budgeted $50 a month for her coffee habit, confident she could stick to it. But a few too many "treat yourself" moments later, she realized she'd spent over $200 on lattes in a single month. The lesson? Sometimes, our best intentions are no match for a perfectly crafted caramel macchiato.

The "Easy" DIY Renovation Disaster:

Jack thought he could save money by renovating his bathroom himself. Armed with YouTube tutorials and an overinflated sense of confidence, he tore down walls, ripped out fixtures, and started plumbing. But what was supposed to be a weekend project turned into a six-month ordeal. He ended up hiring professionals to fix his mess, costing twice as much as if he'd hired them from the start. The takeaway? Sometimes, paying for expertise upfront is cheaper than paying to fix your own mistakes.

The Investment in Imaginary Gold:

Tom got swept up in the latest investment craze: cryptocurrency. He invested his savings in a new, "promising" digital coin, convinced he'd strike it rich. But instead of gold, he ended up with fool's gold. The coin's value plummeted, leaving Tom with a wallet full of worthless digital currency. His wife, meanwhile, invested in a new pair of shoes and came out ahead. The moral? Sometimes, the safest investment is a solid pair of running shoes to run away from get-rich-quick schemes.

The Overzealous Couponing Catastrophe:

Sarah discovered the thrill of extreme couponing and set out to save big on her groceries. She clipped coupons with a fervor, spending hours each week planning her shopping trips. But her first major haul turned into a disaster when she realized she'd misread the fine print and most of her coupons were invalid. Instead of saving money, she ended up paying full price and lugging home 30 cans of tomato soup she didn't need. The lesson?

Sometimes, the devil really is in the details – and in your pantry.

The High-Flying Credit Card Fiasco:

David loved his rewards credit card. He racked up points on everything from groceries to gas, dreaming of the day he'd cash them in for a free vacation. But he forgot one crucial detail: paying off his balance. The interest charges piled up faster than his points, and he ended up deep in debt. His free vacation? A weekend at home, trying to figure out how to pay off his bill. The takeaway? Credit card rewards are great, but they're not worth drowning in debt for.

The Subscription Service Swindle:

Lisa signed up for a free trial of a subscription service, planning to cancel before the charges kicked in. But life got busy, and she forgot. Months later, she discovered she'd been paying for a service she never used. The kicker? She'd signed up with multiple email addresses to get extra free trials, so she was paying for the same service three times. The moral? Free trials aren't free if you forget to cancel – and sometimes, less is more.

The Over-the-Top Wedding Woes:

Jenny and Mark wanted a fairytale wedding and spared no expense. They booked the dream venue, splurged on a designer dress, and hired a live band. But after the big day, they were left with a mountain of debt and a honeymoon budget that stretched only to a weekend staycation. Their marriage started with a sobering lesson: fairytales are expensive, and true love doesn't require a five-figure party. The takeaway? Focus on the marriage, not the wedding – and save some money for the honeymoon.

Tips for Finding Humor in Financial Chaos

Financial chaos can be stressful, but finding humor in the situation can lighten the load and keep you sane. Here are some tips for laughing through the struggles and turning financial disasters into opportunities for growth and hilarity.

Embrace the Absurdity:

Sometimes, the best way to cope with financial stress is to embrace the absurdity of it all. When you're faced with a $500 car repair bill for a vehicle worth $300, or you realize you've spent more on takeout than on rent, just laugh. Life is full of unexpected twists and turns, and finding humor in the ridiculousness can make it all a bit more bearable.

Share Your Stories:

Sharing your financial fails with friends and family can be incredibly therapeutic. Not only does it provide a good laugh, but it also reminds you that everyone makes mistakes. Swap stories of your most embarrassing money moments and learn from each other's experiences. You might even discover that your disaster wasn't so bad after all – or at least, it makes for a great icebreaker at parties.

Celebrate Small Victories:

In the midst of financial chaos, it's important to celebrate the small victories. Did you resist the urge to splurge on a sale? Pat yourself on the back. Managed to cook dinner at home instead of ordering takeout? That's a win. These little triumphs add up and help you stay motivated. Plus, they're a reminder that you're capable of making good financial decisions, even if they sometimes feel few and far between.

Find Humor in Everyday Frugality:

Embrace the humor in everyday frugality. Whether it's repurposing old socks as dust rags or finding creative ways to stretch your grocery budget, there's always a funny side to saving money. Share your quirky frugal hacks with friends and laugh about the lengths you'll go to save a buck. Who knows? You might inspire someone else to embrace their inner cheapskate.

Turn Mishaps into Learning Opportunities:

Every financial misstep is a chance to learn and grow. Instead of beating yourself up over a mistake, look at it as an opportunity to improve your financial savvy. Did you blow your budget on a shopping spree? Learn to recognize your spending triggers. Got burned by a bad investment? Research safer options next time. Each mistake brings valuable lessons that can help you avoid similar pitfalls in the future.

Laugh at Your Old Self:

Look back on your past financial blunders and laugh at how far you've come. Remember when you thought buying that expensive gym membership would make you work out more? Or when you believed you could save money by cutting your own hair? Reflecting on these moments with humor can give you perspective and show you how much you've learned.

Use Humor as a Coping Mechanism:

When financial stress threatens to overwhelm you, use humor as a coping mechanism. Watch a funny movie, read a comedic book, or find a meme that captures your situation perfectly. Laughter releases endorphins and can help you see your problems in a new light. It's not a cure-all, but it's a valuable tool in your stress-relief arsenal.

Create a Financial Fails Journal:

Start a journal to document your financial misadventures. Write down the details of each fail, along with what you learned and how you found humor in the situation. Over time, you'll have a collection of stories that not only make you laugh but also remind you of your resilience and growth. Plus, it's a great way to track your progress and see how far you've come.

Remember, You're Not Alone:

Financial struggles are a universal experience. No matter how unique or embarrassing your financial fail might seem, there's someone out there who's been through something similar. Remembering that you're not alone can help you find solace and laughter in shared experiences. Reach out to friends, join online communities, or read about others' financial journeys to remind yourself that we're all in this together.

Focus on the Bigger Picture:

Finally, keep the bigger picture in mind. Financial missteps are just one part of your journey. They don't define you or determine your future. By focusing on your long-term goals and staying committed to improving your financial health, you can weather the storms and come out stronger on the other side. And along the way, don't forget to laugh at the bumps and detours that make the journey uniquely yours.

Embracing Resilience Through Humor

Financial fails are an inevitable part of life, but they don't have to drag you down. By finding humor in the chaos and learning from your mistakes, you can build resilience and navigate your financial journey with a lighter heart. Here's how to embrace resilience through humor and keep moving forward, no matter how many times you stumble.

Develop a Positive Mindset:

Cultivating a positive mindset can help you navigate financial challenges with grace and humor. Instead of dwelling on the negatives, focus on the opportunities for growth and improvement. A positive outlook makes it easier to find the silver lining in any situation and helps you bounce back more quickly from setbacks.

Practice Gratitude:

Gratitude is a powerful tool for building resilience. Take time each day to reflect on what you're grateful for, even in the midst of financial struggles. Whether it's the support of loved ones, the roof over your head, or the small joys that brighten your day, gratitude shifts your focus from what's lacking to what's abundant. And it's hard to stay down when you're counting your blessings.

Laugh at Life's Ironies:

Life is full of ironies, especially when it comes to money. Embrace these moments with a sense of humor and appreciate the absurdity of it all. Did your car break down the day after you paid off your credit card? Laugh at the timing and remind yourself that you'll handle whatever comes your way. Finding humor in life's ironies can help you stay flexible and adaptable.

Surround Yourself with Support:

Having a strong support network is crucial for resilience. Surround yourself with friends and family who lift you up and share your sense of humor. Lean on them when you're facing financial challenges and let them remind you that you're not alone. Sharing laughs with loved ones can lighten your load and give you the strength to keep going.

Keep Moving Forward:

Resilience is about perseverance and the willingness to keep moving forward, no matter how many times you stumble. Each financial fail is a stepping stone on your path to success. Keep your eyes on your goals, stay flexible, and use humor to navigate the twists and turns. With each step, you're building the resilience and wisdom that will carry you through future challenges.

Turn Challenges into Opportunities:

Every challenge is an opportunity in disguise. When you face financial struggles, look for ways to turn them into opportunities for growth and learning. Did you overspend on a vacation? Use it as a chance to hone your budgeting skills. Struggling to save money? Explore creative ways to boost your income. By reframing challenges as opportunities, you can approach them with a sense of curiosity and humor.

Celebrate Your Progress:

Take time to celebrate your progress, no matter how small. Every step forward is a victory, whether it's paying off a debt, sticking to a budget, or finding a new side hustle. Celebrating your achievements, no matter how minor, reinforces your sense of accomplishment and motivates you to keep pushing forward. Plus, it's a great excuse to treat yourself – within your budget, of course.

Embrace Imperfection:

No one is perfect, and financial journeys are rarely smooth. Embrace your imperfections and accept that you'll make mistakes along the way. Instead of striving for perfection, focus on making progress and learning from your experiences. Embracing imperfection allows you to approach your finances with a sense of humor and resilience, knowing that you're doing your best.

Find Joy in the Journey:

The financial journey is a marathon, not a sprint. Find joy in the process and appreciate the lessons and experiences that come your way. Whether it's the satisfaction of a well-balanced budget or the hilarity of a financial mishap, each moment contributes to your growth. By finding joy in the journey, you can stay motivated and resilient, no matter what challenges you face.

Keep Laughing:

Laughter truly is the best medicine. It lightens your mood, reduces stress, and helps you see your problems in a new light. Whenever you're facing financial struggles, find a reason to laugh – whether it's at the absurdity of the situation, the lessons you've learned, or the shared experiences with others. Laughter connects us, heals us, and reminds us that no matter how tough things get, we can always find a reason to smile.

In this chapter, we've shared hilarious accounts of financial missteps and explored tips for finding humor in the midst of financial chaos. From budget blunders to DIY disasters, these stories remind us that we're not alone in our struggles. By embracing humor, sharing our experiences, and learning from our mistakes, we can navigate the ups and downs of financial life with resilience and a smile. So, keep laughing, keep learning, and remember that every financial fail is just another chapter in your story – one that you can turn into a comedy if you choose.

6 FINDING JOY IN THE JOURNEY

As we reach the end of our journey through Brokesville, it's time to pause and reflect on the unexpected joys and laughs that come with financial difficulties. Yes, being broke can be stressful, frustrating, and downright absurd at times. But amidst the chaos and penny-pinching, there's a wealth of moments that bring us joy and remind us that life's richness isn't measured by the balance in our bank accounts.

From the laughter shared over a kitchen table covered in DIY mishaps to the sense of triumph when you finally make that Ramen recipe taste gourmet, these are the moments that add color and texture to our lives. Financial struggles often force us to get creative, to think outside the box, and to find humor in places we never thought to look. It's in these small victories and silly anecdotes that we discover the true essence of resilience and joy.

As you navigate the road to financial stability, remember to keep smiling and joking. Let your sense of humor be your compass, guiding you through the rough patches with a light heart and a hearty laugh. Embrace the ridiculousness of your financial misadventures, and don't be afraid to share your stories with others. Laughter is a powerful tool for connection and healing, and it turns even the toughest times into memories worth cherishing.

So, whether you're stretching pennies or conquering side hustles, finding joy in the journey is about embracing the ups and downs with a smile. Keep laughing at life's absurdities, celebrating your progress, and remembering that even if you're broke, you're rich in spirit and surrounded by moments of unexpected happiness. Here's to finding joy in every twist and turn, and to the brighter, more financially stable days ahead. Keep laughing, keep living, and above all, keep finding joy in the journey.

7 TOOLS OF VICTORY

Creating a comprehensive set of worksheets, logs, assessments, and budgets can help manage and plan finances effectively, especially when resources are tight. Below is a collection of tools designed to assist in various aspects of financial management and planning.

1. Budget Worksheets

Monthly Budget Worksheet

Category	Budgeted Amount	Actual Amount	Difference
Income			
Salary			
Side Hustles			
Other Income			
Total Income			
Expenses			
Rent/Mortgage			
Utilities			
Groceries			
Transportation			
Insurance			

Category	Budgeted Amount	Actual Amount	Difference
Entertainment			
Savings			
Debt Payments			
Miscellaneous			
Total Expenses			
Net Balance			

2. Financial Logs

Daily Spending Log

Date	Item/Purchase	Category	Amount
Total			

3. Financial Assessments

Financial Health Check

Assessment Area	Questions	Yes/No Notes
Income Stability	Do you have a stable source of income?	
	Do you have multiple streams of income?	
Savings	Do you have an emergency fund?	
	Are you saving at least 10% of your income?	
Debt Management	Are you able to make your debt payments on time?	
	Are your total debt payments less than 30% of your income?	
Spending Habits	Do you track your daily expenses?	
	Are you able to stick to your budget consistently?	
Future Planning	Do you have a retirement plan in place?	

Assessment Area	Questions	Yes/No Notes
	Are you saving for future goals (e.g., home, education)?	
Insurance	Do you have health insurance?	
	Do you have sufficient coverage for life and property?	
Overall Financial Health	Do you feel confident in managing your finances?	

4. Savings Goals Worksheet

Savings Goals Tracker

Goal	Target Amount	Current Amount	Monthly Contribution	Target Date	Notes
Emergency Fund					
Vacation Fund					
New Car					
Home Purchase					
Education					
Total					

5. Meal Planning and Grocery Budget

Weekly Meal Planner

Day	Breakfast	Lunch	Dinner	Snacks	Grocery List
Monday					
Tuesday					
Wednesday					
Thursday					
Friday					
Saturday					
Sunday					

6. Debt Reduction Plan

Debt Payment Tracker

Creditor	Total Debt	Interest Rate	Minimum Payment	Additional Payment	New Balance

Total

7. Income Tracker

Income Tracking Sheet

Source	Expected Amount	Actual Amount	Difference Notes
Salary			
Side Hustles			
Freelance Work			
Investments			
Other			
Total			

8. Personal Financial Goals

Financial Goals Worksheet

Goal	Description	Target Date	Steps to Achieve	Progress
Build Emergency Fund	Save $1,000 for emergencies		Set up automatic transfers, reduce expenses	
Pay Off Credit Card	Pay off $2,000 in credit card debt		Increase payments, use extra income	
Save for Vacation	Save $500 for a trip		Save $50 per month, cut back on dining out	
Retirement Savings	Contribute $3,000 to IRA		Set up monthly contributions, review investments	

9. Utility and Bill Tracker

Monthly Bill Tracker

Bill	Due Date	Amount	Paid	Notes
Rent/Mortgage				
Electricity				
Water				
Gas				
Internet				
Phone				
Insurance				
Subscriptions				
Total				

10. Income vs. Expense Summary

Monthly Summary

Category	Income	Expenses	Difference
Salary			
Side Hustles			
Freelance Work			
Investments			
Other Income			
Rent/Mortgage			
Utilities			
Groceries			
Transportation			
Insurance			
Entertainment			
Savings			
Debt Payments			
Miscellaneous			

Category   Income Expenses Difference

Total

8 POOR MAN'S COOKBOOK

35 Recipes with 5 Ingredients or Less

Welcome to the Poor Man's Cookbook, your ultimate guide to delicious, budget-friendly meals made with just five ingredients or less. Whether you're navigating tight finances or simply looking for quick and easy recipes, this collection has something for everyone. These recipes are simple, satisfying, and proof that you don't need a lot of money – or ingredients – to create a great meal. So grab your pantry staples and let's get cooking!

With these 35 simple recipes, you can enjoy a variety of delicious meals without breaking the bank or spending hours in the kitchen. Each recipe uses just five ingredients or less, proving that you can eat well even on a tight budget. Happy cooking!

Breakfast

Banana Pancakes

1. **Ingredients**: 1 ripe banana, 2 eggs, 1/2 cup flour, 1/4 cup milk, 1 tsp baking powder.
2. **Instructions**: Mash the banana in a bowl. Add eggs and whisk until combined. Stir in flour, milk, and baking powder until smooth. Cook on a greased skillet over medium heat until golden brown on both sides.

Avocado Toast

1. **Ingredients**: 1 ripe avocado, 2 slices of bread, salt, pepper, lemon juice.
2. **Instructions**: Toast the bread. Mash the avocado with a fork and season with salt, pepper, and a squeeze of lemon juice. Spread the avocado mixture on the toast.

Yogurt Parfait

1. **Ingredients**: 1 cup yogurt, 1/2 cup granola, 1/2 cup fresh berries, 1 tbsp honey.
2. **Instructions**: Layer yogurt, granola, and berries in a glass or bowl. Drizzle with honey and enjoy.

Oatmeal with Peanut Butter and Banana

1. **Ingredients**: 1 cup rolled oats, 2 cups water, 1 banana (sliced), 2 tbsp peanut butter.
2. **Instructions****: Cook oats in water according to package instructions. Top with sliced banana and a dollop of peanut butter.

Egg and Cheese Breakfast Burrito

1. **Ingredients**: 2 eggs, 1 tortilla, 1/4 cup shredded cheese, salt, pepper.
2. **Instructions**: Scramble the eggs with salt and pepper. Place them in a tortilla, sprinkle with cheese, and roll it up.

Snacks and Sides

Garlic Parmesan Popcorn

1. **Ingredients**: 1/2 cup popcorn kernels, 2 tbsp olive oil, 1/4 cup grated Parmesan cheese, 1 tsp garlic powder, salt.
2. **Instructions**: Pop the kernels in oil over medium heat. Toss with Parmesan, garlic powder, and salt.

Cucumber and Hummus

1. **Ingredients**: 1 cucumber, 1 cup hummus.

2. **Instructions**: Slice the cucumber into rounds and serve with hummus for dipping.

Caprese Skewers

1. **Ingredients**: Cherry tomatoes, fresh mozzarella balls, fresh basil leaves, balsamic glaze.
2. **Instructions**: Skewer tomatoes, mozzarella, and basil. Drizzle with balsamic glaze.

Apple Slices with Peanut Butter

1. **Ingredients**: 1 apple, 2 tbsp peanut butter.
2. **Instructions**: Slice the apple and serve with peanut butter for dipping.

Cheesy Garlic Bread

1. **Ingredients**: 1 baguette, 2 tbsp butter, 1 tsp garlic powder, 1/2 cup shredded mozzarella cheese.
2. **Instructions**: Slice the baguette, spread with butter mixed with garlic powder, and top with cheese. Bake at 350°F (175°C) until cheese is melted and bubbly.

Soups and Salads

Tomato Basil Soup

1. **Ingredients**: 1 can (28 oz) crushed tomatoes, 1 cup vegetable broth, 1/4 cup heavy cream, fresh basil, salt.

2. **Instructions**: Combine tomatoes and broth in a pot and bring to a simmer. Stir in cream and chopped basil. Season with salt.

Simple Green Salad

1. **Ingredients**: Mixed greens, 1 cucumber (sliced), 1/2 red onion (sliced), 1/4 cup olive oil, 2 tbsp vinegar.
2. **Instructions**: Toss greens, cucumber, and onion. Dress with olive oil and vinegar.

Chicken Noodle Soup

1. **Ingredients**: 2 cups chicken broth, 1 cup cooked chicken (shredded), 1 cup egg noodles, 1 carrot (sliced), salt, and pepper.
2. **Instructions**: Combine broth, chicken, and carrot in a pot. Bring to a boil, add noodles, and cook until tender. Season with salt and pepper.

Greek Salad

1. **Ingredients**: 1 cucumber (diced), 1 tomato (diced), 1/4 cup feta cheese (crumbled), 1/4 cup black olives, olive oil.
2. **Instructions**: Toss cucumber, tomato, feta, and olives. Drizzle with olive oil.

Potato Leek Soup

1. **Ingredients**: 2 potatoes (peeled and diced), 2 leeks (sliced), 2 cups vegetable broth, 1/2 cup milk, salt, and pepper.

2. **Instructions**: Sauté leeks in a pot until soft. Add potatoes and broth, and simmer until tender. Blend until smooth and stir in milk. Season with salt and pepper.

Main Dishes

Spaghetti Aglio e Olio

1. **Ingredients**: 8 oz spaghetti, 1/4 cup olive oil, 4 garlic cloves (sliced), red pepper flakes, Parmesan cheese.
2. **Instructions**: Cook spaghetti until al dente. Sauté garlic in olive oil with red pepper flakes until golden. Toss with pasta and sprinkle with Parmesan.

Chicken Stir-Fry

1. **Ingredients**: 1 chicken breast (sliced), 1 bell pepper (sliced), 1 cup broccoli florets, 2 tbsp soy sauce, 1 tbsp sesame oil.
2. **Instructions**: Sauté chicken in sesame oil until cooked through. Add vegetables and soy sauce, and cook until tender.

Grilled Cheese Sandwich

1. **Ingredients**: 2 slices of bread, 2 slices of cheese, 2 tbsp butter.
2. **Instructions**: Butter one side of each bread slice. Place cheese between bread with buttered sides out. Cook in a skillet over medium heat until golden brown and cheese is melted.

Tuna Salad

1. **Ingredients**: 1 can tuna, 2 tbsp mayonnaise, 1 celery stalk (chopped), 1 tbsp lemon juice, salt, and pepper.
2. **Instructions**: Mix tuna, mayonnaise, celery, and lemon juice. Season with salt and pepper.

Vegetable Quesadilla

1. **Ingredients**: 2 tortillas, 1 cup mixed vegetables (frozen or fresh), 1/2 cup shredded cheese.
2. **Instructions**: Sauté vegetables until tender. Place one tortilla in a skillet, top with vegetables and cheese, and cover with the other tortilla. Cook until golden brown, then flip and cook the other side.

Baked Chicken Thighs

1. **Ingredients**: 4 chicken thighs, 2 tbsp olive oil, 1 tsp garlic powder, salt, and pepper.
2. **Instructions**: Preheat oven to 375°F (190°C). Rub chicken with olive oil, garlic powder, salt, and pepper. Bake for 35-40 minutes or until cooked through.

Easy Beef Tacos

1. **Ingredients**: 1 lb ground beef, 1 packet taco seasoning, 8 taco shells, 1 cup shredded lettuce, 1/2 cup salsa.
2. **Instructions**: Cook beef in a skillet until browned. Add taco seasoning and prepare according to the package. Serve in taco shells with lettuce and salsa.

Black Bean Burgers

1. **Ingredients**: 1 can black beans (drained and mashed), 1/2 cup breadcrumbs, 1 egg, 1 tsp cumin, salt, and pepper.
2. **Instructions**: Mix all ingredients and form into patties. Cook in a skillet over medium heat until browned on both sides.

Pasta Primavera

1. **Ingredients**: 8 oz pasta, 1 cup mixed vegetables, 2 tbsp olive oil, 1 clove garlic (minced), Parmesan cheese.
2. **Instructions**: Cook pasta until al dente. Sauté vegetables and garlic in olive oil until tender. Toss with pasta and sprinkle with Parmesan.

Baked Salmon

1. **Ingredients**: 2 salmon fillets, 2 tbsp olive oil, 1 lemon (sliced), salt, and pepper.
2. **Instructions**: Preheat oven to 375°F (190°C). Place salmon on a baking sheet, drizzle with olive oil, and top with lemon slices. Season with salt and pepper. Bake for 15-20 minutes or until cooked through.

Stuffed Peppers

1. **Ingredients**: 4 bell peppers (tops removed), 1 cup cooked rice, 1 cup ground beef (cooked), 1/2 cup tomato sauce, shredded cheese.
2. **Instructions**: Mix rice, beef, and tomato sauce. Stuff peppers with the mixture, top with cheese, and bake at 375°F (190°C) for 30 minutes.

Egg Fried Rice

1. **Ingredients**: 2 cups cooked rice, 2 eggs, 1 cup mixed vegetables, 2 tbsp soy sauce, 1 tbsp vegetable oil.
2. **Instructions**: Heat oil in a skillet. Scramble eggs, add rice and vegetables, and cook until heated through. Stir in soy sauce.

Ham and Cheese Roll-Ups

1. **Ingredients**: 4 slices of deli ham, 4 slices of cheese, 4 tortillas.
2. **Instructions**: Place a slice of ham and cheese on each tortilla. Roll up and serve.

Baked Potatoes

1. **Ingredients**: 4 potatoes, 2 tbsp olive oil, salt, pepper, toppings of your choice (e.g., sour cream, chives, cheese).
2. **Instructions**: Preheat oven to 400°F (200°C). Rub potatoes with olive oil, salt, and pepper. Bake for 45-60 minutes until tender. Add your favorite toppings.

Simple Chicken Alfredo

1. **Ingredients**: 1 chicken breast (sliced), 8 oz fettuccine, 1 cup heavy cream, 1/2 cup Parmesan cheese, 1 tbsp butter.
2. **Instructions**: Cook fettuccine according to the package. Sauté chicken in butter until cooked through. Add cream and cheese, stir until thickened, and toss with pasta.

Desserts

Peanut Butter Cookies

1. **Ingredients**: 1 cup peanut butter, 1 cup sugar, 1 egg.
2. **Instructions**: Preheat oven to 350°F (175°C). Mix all ingredients until combined. Drop spoonfuls onto a baking sheet and flatten with a fork. Bake for 10-12 minutes.

Banana Ice Cream

1. **Ingredients**: 2 ripe bananas (frozen), 1 tbsp peanut butter.
2. **Instructions**: Blend frozen bananas and peanut butter until smooth. Serve immediately or freeze for a firmer texture.

Chocolate Mug Cake

1. **Ingredients**: 1/4 cup flour, 1/4 cup sugar, 2 tbsp cocoa powder, 3 tbsp milk, 2 tbsp vegetable oil.
2. **Instructions**: Mix all ingredients in a microwave-safe mug until smooth. Microwave for 1-2 minutes until cooked through.

Fruit Salad

1. **Ingredients**: 1 cup strawberries (sliced), 1 cup blueberries, 1 cup pineapple (diced), 1 cup grapes.
2. **Instructions**: Combine all fruits in a bowl and toss gently.

Rice Krispie Treats

1. **Ingredients**: 3 cups Rice Krispies cereal, 3 tbsp butter, 1 package (10 oz) marshmallows.
2. **Instructions**: Melt butter in a pot, add marshmallows, and stir until melted. Remove from heat and stir in cereal until coated. Press into a greased pan and cool before cutting.

Home Made Beauty Products

Homemade Facial Cleanser: Mix equal parts honey and coconut oil to create a gentle cleanser that removes dirt and makeup while moisturizing the skin.

DIY Face Scrub: Combine brown sugar with olive oil or coconut oil to create a nourishing exfoliating scrub that sloughs away dead skin cells.

Soothing Oatmeal Mask: Blend rolled oats with water to create a paste, then apply it to the skin for a calming and hydrating face mask.

Refreshing Cucumber Toner: Blend cucumber slices with water, strain the mixture, and use it as a cooling toner to refresh and tone the skin.

Moisturizing Avocado Mask: Mash ripe avocado with a teaspoon of honey to create a hydrating and nourishing face mask that leaves skin soft and smooth.

Brightening Lemon Scrub: Mix lemon juice with granulated sugar and a bit of coconut oil to create a brightening scrub that helps even out skin tone and texture.

Hydrating Aloe Vera Gel: Use pure aloe vera gel straight from the plant to soothe and hydrate the skin, especially after sun exposure.

Energizing Coffee Scrub: Combine used coffee grounds with coconut oil to create a invigorating body scrub that helps exfoliate and smooth the skin.

Calming Lavender Bath Soak: Add a few drops of lavender essential oil to a warm bath along with Epsom salts to create a relaxing and calming soak for tired muscles and stressed skin.

DIY Lip Balm: Melt together equal parts coconut oil, shea butter, and beeswax, then pour into small containers to create a nourishing lip balm.

Gentle Honey Mask: Mix raw honey with a splash of apple cider vinegar to create a gentle mask that helps clarify and balance the skin.

Soothing Aloe Vera Sunburn Relief: Apply pure aloe vera gel to sunburned skin to help soothe inflammation and promote healing.

DIY Body Butter: Whip together shea butter, cocoa butter, and coconut oil to create a luxurious body butter that deeply moisturizes dry skin.

Antioxidant Green Tea Toner: Brew green tea, let it cool, and use it as a toner to help tighten pores and reduce inflammation.

Acne-Fighting Tea Tree Spot Treatment: Dilute tea tree essential oil with a carrier oil like jojoba oil, then apply it directly to blemishes to help reduce inflammation and fight acne-causing bacteria.

Home Made DIY Home Decor Ideas

Wall Art: Create your own paintings, prints, or wall hangings using canvas, paint, or fabric.

Gallery Wall: Curate a collection of photos, artwork, and other decorative items to display on a wall in a cohesive arrangement.

Upcycled Furniture: Repurpose old furniture with a fresh coat of paint, new hardware, or creative embellishments.

Repurposed Mason Jars: Turn mason jars into vases, candle holders, or storage containers with paint, twine, or decorative accents.

Decorative Pillows: Sew or no-sew decorative pillow covers using fabric remnants, old clothing, or thrifted fabrics.

Macramé Wall Hangings: Learn macramé techniques to create intricate wall hangings using rope or yarn.

Terrariums: Build your own terrariums using glass containers, soil, rocks, and small plants like succulents or air plants.

Accent Walls: Paint or wallpaper one wall in a room to create a focal point and add visual interest.

DIY Shelving: Build custom shelves using reclaimed wood, crates, or metal piping for a unique storage solution.

Stenciled Patterns: Use stencils to add patterns or designs to walls, furniture, or fabric surfaces.

String Art: Create geometric or abstract designs by hammering nails into wood and wrapping string or embroidery floss around them.

Photo Collages: Arrange and frame photos in a collage format to create personalized wall art.

Fabric Wall Hangings: Stretch fabric over a wooden frame or embroidery hoop to create fabric wall art.

Dip-Dyeing: Update plain textiles like curtains, pillow covers, or napkins with dip-dyeing techniques.

Pallet Projects: Repurpose wooden pallets into furniture pieces like coffee tables, shelves, or outdoor seating.

Chalkboard Paint: Transform a wall, door, or surface into a chalkboard for doodling, writing notes, or displaying art.

Curtain Tiebacks: Create unique curtain tiebacks using rope, tassels, or vintage doorknobs.

DIY Headboard: Build a custom headboard using reclaimed wood, fabric, or even old doors.

Copper Pipe Creations: Use copper pipes to create modern, industrial-inspired shelves, towel racks, or curtain rods.

Floating Shelves: Install floating shelves to display decorative items, books, or plants without visible brackets.

Home Made Kids Crafts and Activities

Paper Plate Animals: Turn paper plates into cute animals by painting them and adding details like ears, eyes, and noses with construction paper.

Sock Puppets: Create playful sock puppets using old socks, buttons, yarn, and felt for eyes, noses, and mouths.

DIY Slime: Make homemade slime using glue, borax, and food coloring for endless sensory fun.

Tissue Paper Flowers: Craft colorful tissue paper flowers by layering and folding tissue paper, then securing them with pipe cleaners.

Salt Dough Creations: Mix flour, salt, and water to create salt dough, then sculpt it into shapes, ornaments, or handprint keepsakes.

Painted Rocks: Decorate smooth rocks with acrylic paint to create story stones, garden markers, or paperweights.

Popsicle Stick Creations: Build structures, animals, or vehicles using popsicle sticks and glue.

DIY Playdough: Make your own playdough using flour, salt, water, and food coloring, then let the kids mold and shape it into whatever they imagine.

Finger Painting: Encourage creativity with finger painting using washable paint and large sheets of paper or cardboard.

Homemade Bird Feeders: Craft simple bird feeders using pinecones, peanut butter, and birdseed, then hang them outside to attract feathered friends.

Paper Bag Puppets: Decorate paper bags with markers, crayons, and googly eyes to make custom puppets for imaginative play.

DIY Musical Instruments: Create homemade instruments like shakers, drums, or guitars using household items like rice-filled containers, pots, and rubber bands.

Origami: Introduce kids to the art of paper folding with easy origami projects like paper airplanes, animals, or simple shapes.

Bubble Wands: Fashion bubble wands using pipe cleaners bent into various shapes, then dip them into homemade bubble solution for bubble-blowing fun.

Button Art: Sort and arrange colorful buttons to create mosaic-like artwork on paper or cardboard.

Homemade Playdough: Mix together flour, salt, cream of tartar, water, and food coloring to create homemade playdough in any color imaginable.

Paper Bag Masks: Cut eye and mouth holes in paper bags, then let kids decorate them with paint, markers, feathers, and more to make their own masks.

Nature Collages: Go on a nature walk to collect leaves, flowers, and other natural materials, then use them to create beautiful collages.

DIY Friendship Bracelets: Teach kids basic weaving techniques using embroidery floss to create colorful friendship bracelets for themselves and their friends.

Recycled Art Projects: Encourage eco-friendly creativity by using recycled materials like cardboard tubes, egg cartons, and cereal boxes to make sculptures, collages, and more.

Cute and Unique Ways to Save Money

Saving money doesn't have to be a tedious chore; it can be a fun and creative adventure! Here are some cute and unique ways to trim your expenses and boost your savings without feeling deprived. Each of these tips adds a touch of charm and novelty to the mundane task of saving, turning it into an enjoyable part of your daily routine.

1. Envelope Challenge with a Twist

Instead of the traditional envelope budgeting method, turn it into a fun game. Write different saving amounts on 52 envelopes (one for each week of the year) and decorate them with cute stickers or drawings. Shuffle the envelopes and each week, draw one at random. Whatever amount is written on the envelope, set that money aside for your savings. By the end of the year, you'll have a nice stash without the monotony of a fixed weekly amount.

2. Round-Up Piggy Bank

Transform your spare change into savings with a digital round-up piggy bank. Every time you make a purchase, round up the amount to the nearest dollar and save the difference. For example, if you spend $4.75, round up to $5 and save the extra 25 cents. Use an app that automatically does this for you, or keep a jar at home and manually add your rounded-up change. It's a cute and effortless way to build savings without even noticing.

3. 52-Week Savings Jar

Create a cute savings jar and label it with the weeks of the year. Start by saving $1 in the first week, $2 in the second week, and so on until you reach $52 in the last week. By the end of the year, you'll have saved $1,378! Decorate your jar with ribbons, stickers, or paint to make it visually appealing and keep it in a place where you can see your progress and stay motivated.

4. Coupon Clip Art

Turn couponing into an art project. Instead of just clipping coupons, create a scrapbook where you can paste them in a visually appealing way. Organize your coupons by category and decorate the pages with drawings or stickers. This makes the process of finding and using coupons more enjoyable and turns a mundane task into a creative endeavor.

5. The Penny Challenge

This adorable savings plan starts with saving just a penny on the first day, two pennies on the second day, and so on. By the end of the year, you'll have saved $667.95! Keep a pretty jar or piggy bank to collect your pennies and watch your savings grow each day. It's a tiny daily commitment that adds up to a significant amount over time.

6. Friendship Fund

Start a savings challenge with your friends! Agree to save a certain amount each week or month, and keep each other accountable. Share your progress and celebrate milestones together. To make it more fun, plan a small treat or outing for everyone once you reach a collective goal. It's a great way to bond and stay motivated while building your savings.

7. DIY No-Spend Weekends

Declare one weekend a month as a "No-Spend Weekend."
Instead of going out and spending money, plan fun and free
activities at home. Host a potluck dinner, have a movie
marathon with homemade popcorn, or go on a nature hike.
Document your adventures with photos or a journal entry to
remember how enjoyable and fulfilling your no-spend
weekends can be.

8. DIY Gifts and Cards

Embrace your crafty side and make your own gifts and cards
for birthdays, holidays, or special occasions. Not only will you
save money, but your handmade creations will be cherished
more than store-bought items. From baked goods to knitted
scarves or personalized photo albums, the possibilities are
endless and your thoughtfulness will shine through.

9. Upcycle and Repurpose

Before you throw anything away, think about how you can
repurpose it. Turn old T-shirts into cleaning rags, glass jars
into storage containers, or cereal boxes into drawer dividers.
This not only saves money but also adds a touch of creativity
and sustainability to your home. Get the whole family involved
in upcycling projects to make it a fun and educational activity.

10. Digital Detox Days

Set aside one day a week to unplug from all digital devices.
Spend time outdoors, read a book, or engage in hobbies that
don't require electronics. This not only saves on electricity but
also helps reduce the temptation to shop online or spend
money on digital entertainment. It's a refreshing way to
recharge and enjoy simple pleasures.

11. Frugal Fashion Swap

Organize a clothing swap party with friends. Everyone brings clothes, accessories, or shoes they no longer want, and you can trade items with each other. It's a fantastic way to refresh your wardrobe without spending a dime. Plus, you'll get to socialize and maybe discover some new fashion gems that your friends were ready to part with.

12. Recipe Roulette

Instead of dining out, make meal planning fun with "Recipe Roulette." Write down the names of all your favorite recipes on slips of paper and put them in a jar. Each week, draw a slip from the jar to decide what you'll cook. This adds an element of surprise to your meals and encourages you to use ingredients you already have, saving you money on groceries and reducing food waste.

13. Cute Coin Collection

Turn saving spare change into a fun activity. Get a cute coin bank (like one shaped like a pig, owl, or whatever tickles your fancy) and challenge yourself to fill it up. Once it's full, take it to the bank and deposit your savings. Watching your coin bank fill up can be surprisingly satisfying and motivating.

14. Memory Jar

Instead of spending money on entertainment, start a "Memory Jar." Whenever you have a memorable experience, write it down on a piece of paper and put it in the jar. At the end of the year, read through all the memories you've collected. This helps you focus on the joy of experiences rather than material things and can be a delightful way to reflect on your year.

15. Subscription Audit

Go through all your subscriptions and services to identify any that you don't use or can live without. Canceling unused subscriptions is an easy way to cut down on monthly expenses. To make the process more enjoyable, turn it into a "Subscription Scavenger Hunt" and reward yourself with a small treat for every unnecessary subscription you cancel.

16. Garden and Grow

Start a small garden, even if it's just a few pots on your windowsill. Growing your own herbs, vegetables, or fruits can save you money on groceries and add a fresh, homegrown touch to your meals. Plus, gardening is a relaxing and rewarding hobby that brings a bit of nature into your home.

17. Beauty on a Budget

Create your own beauty products at home. From face masks and scrubs to hair treatments, there are plenty of DIY recipes that use simple ingredients you probably already have in your kitchen. It's a fun and cost-effective way to pamper yourself without breaking the bank.

18. Seasonal Scavenger Hunts

Instead of spending money on outings, plan seasonal scavenger hunts. Create a list of items or experiences to find or do, like spotting certain types of flowers in spring, collecting colorful leaves in fall, or finding holiday decorations in winter. It's a delightful way to explore your surroundings and enjoy the beauty of each season.

19. Thrift Store Treasure Hunts

Make a game out of shopping at thrift stores. Set a budget and see who can find the best items for the least amount of money. Whether you're looking for clothes, home decor, or books, thrift stores are full of hidden treasures. This turns shopping into a fun adventure and helps you save money while supporting sustainable practices.

20. Library Lovers

Become a regular at your local library. Borrow books, movies, and even games instead of buying them. Many libraries also offer free workshops, events, and classes. It's a treasure trove of resources and entertainment that's often overlooked. Plus, visiting the library can be a cozy and quiet way to spend an afternoon.

21. Crafty Cash Savings

Turn your love for crafts into a way to save money. Instead of buying new decorations or gifts, create them yourself. From homemade candles and soaps to knitted scarves and hand-painted signs, there are endless possibilities for DIY projects. It's a charming way to personalize your space and gifts while keeping your spending in check.

22. Meal Prep Magic

Dedicate one day a week to meal prepping. Cook and portion out your meals in advance to avoid the temptation of dining out or ordering takeout. Use cute containers or jars to store your meals and make the process more enjoyable. It's a practical way to save money and eat healthier, all while having fun in the kitchen.

23. Energy-Saving Dance Party

Turn energy savings into a party. Have a weekly "lights out" dance party where you use minimal electricity – light some candles, play music on a battery-powered device, and dance around your living room. It's a playful way to reduce your energy bills and have a blast doing it.

24. Pet Savings Jar

If you have pets, start a savings jar specifically for their expenses. Decorate the jar with their photos and add a small amount of money each week. This can help cover unexpected vet bills or spoil them with new toys and treats. It's a cute way to budget for your furry friends and ensure you're prepared for any pet-related expenses.

25. Virtual Travel Adventures

Save on travel costs by exploring the world virtually. Use online resources to "visit" different countries, learn about their cultures, and even try their recipes at home. Plan a themed night with food, music, and activities from your chosen destination. It's a fun way to satisfy your wanderlust without spending a fortune on plane tickets.

26. DIY Spa Day

Create a spa experience at home with DIY treatments. Make your own face masks, foot scrubs, and bath bombs using simple ingredients. Light some candles, play soothing music, and enjoy a relaxing spa day without the hefty price tag. It's a luxurious way to treat yourself while staying within budget.

27. Entertainment Swap

Swap books, movies, and games with friends instead of buying new ones. This not only saves money but also introduces you to new entertainment options you might not have discovered otherwise. Organize a regular swap event and enjoy the variety without the expense.

28. Potluck Parties

Host potluck parties where everyone brings a dish. This not only spreads out the cost of food but also creates a diverse and delicious spread. It's a wonderful way to socialize and enjoy a variety of dishes without the burden of cooking and paying for everything yourself.

29. DIY Cleaning Products

Make your own cleaning products using ingredients like vinegar, baking soda, and essential oils. They're often cheaper and safer than store-bought alternatives, and you can customize the scents and formulas to your liking. Plus, there's something satisfying about cleaning your home with products you made yourself.

30. Declutter and Sell

Declutter your home and sell items you no longer need. Whether it's clothes, electronics, or home goods, you can turn your unwanted items into cash. Use online marketplaces or have a garage sale, and enjoy the dual benefits of a tidier space and extra money in your pocket.

31. Cash-Only Weekends

Challenge yourself to spend only cash for a weekend. Leave your cards at home and take a set amount of cash for all your expenses. This helps you become more mindful of your spending and makes it easier to stick to your budget. Plus, there's a certain old-school charm in handling physical money.

32. Nature's Gym

Cancel your gym membership and use the great outdoors as your workout space. Go for hikes, runs, or even follow workout videos in your backyard. Nature offers endless opportunities for physical activity, and it's completely free. Plus, exercising outside can be refreshing and invigorating.

33. Gratitude Journal

Start a gratitude journal where you write down things you're thankful for each day. This helps shift your focus from what you lack to what you have, fostering contentment and reducing the urge to spend money on unnecessary things. It's a simple practice that can have a profound impact on your happiness and financial well-being.

34. Skill Share

Barter your skills with friends and neighbors. Offer to teach a skill you have in exchange for something you need. Whether it's cooking lessons for gardening tips or tech help for car repairs, skill sharing can save you money and build community connections.

35. Homemade Treats

Instead of buying expensive snacks and treats, make them at home. Bake cookies, make granola bars, or prepare your own trail mix. It's often cheaper and healthier than store-bought options, and you can enjoy the process of creating delicious treats in your kitchen.